SOCIAL MEDIA MARKETING MASTERY 2025

THE FOOLPROOF GUIDE TO BUILDING WEALTH AND SUCCESS ONLINE

KALEIGH S GRACIA

COPYRIGHT

Disclaimer:
This publication is intended to provide accurate and authoritative information regarding the subject matter covered. Every effort has been made to ensure that the content is up-to-date, accurate,

For permissions, please contact:
Kaleighgracia@gmail.com]

First Edition: 2025
Printed in [united state of America]

TABLE OF CONTENT

INTRODUCTION
Greetings from the Social Media Marketing Universe

Greetings from a world where success is only a few clicks away and chances are endless. Social media is now a worldwide marketplace, a community builder, and a potent instrument for making a significant impact—it's no longer just a place to share pictures or keep in touch with pals. Everyone, from startups to multinational corporations, is using social media to expand their brand, engage with customers, and accomplish previously unheard-of levels of success.

Your golden passport to this

dynamic and lively ecology is this guide. This book will help you discover the secrets of social media marketing and change your life, regardless of whether you're a total novice, small company owner, or someone trying to reinvent your profession.

Why Social Media Will Be 2025's Goldmine

A turning point in the digital era will occur around 2025. With more than 4.9 billion users globally, social media platforms have emerged as the hub for both business and human contact. The opportunities are boundless, ranging from the emergence of influencer marketing to the expanding significance of short-form video content.

Social media is an equalizer, not only for large enterprises. Making an impression doesn't require a large budget or a marketing degree. Even the tiniest accounts may develop into prosperous empires with the correct approach, perseverance, and inventiveness.

Imagine being able to use your living room to reach millions of potential clients, having the capacity to make money from your passion, or having the opportunity to develop a personal brand that exudes authority and trust. All of this and more is available on social media. The only issue is, are you prepared to take advantage of this chance?

How This Guide Will Help You Become an Expert in Marketing

One step at a time, this book will guide you from a novice to an expert in social media marketing. You will discover how to create engaging content, interact with your audience, and become an expert on the nuances of platforms like as YouTube, Instagram, X (previously Twitter), and TikTok.

This guide demystifies social

media marketing with simple instructions, real-world examples, and tried-and-true tactics. You'll learn how to assess progress, set reasonable goals, and adjust to shifting trends. You'll discover how to produce impactful content that engages, converts, and produces outcomes in addition to learning how to post.

You will not only comprehend social media at the conclusion of this voyage, but you will also be an owner of it. You'll have the self-assurance, know-how, and resources necessary to realize your goals and become one of the people who have fully realized the promise of the digital world.

The future has here, and this is where your success journey starts. Let's get started!

SECTION 1: BEGINNING Social Media Marketing Fundamentals

Social media marketing: what is it?

The art and science of leveraging social media sites like Facebook, Instagram, TikTok, X (previously Twitter), and others to engage with your audience, develop your brand, and eventually encourage lucrative behavior is known as social media marketing. Social media has developed into a major force in communication and business in the modern day, moving beyond its initial usage as a tool for socializing. By utilizing this reach, social media marketing gives both individuals and companies a direct connection to millions of people worldwide. In addition to connecting and interacting with your audience, it enables you to convert these exchanges into significant commercial outcomes, such as increasing website traffic, brand exposure, or sales. It's the most effective strategy for influencing and building enduring connections with your clients.

Comprehending Platforms and Their Objectives

Each social media site has its own audience, features, and goals. Knowing what each one delivers and how it fits with your objectives is essential for success.

Facebook is the best platform for creating communities, disseminating longer-form content, and executing targeted paid advertising campaigns. Instagram's emphasis on visuals makes it ideal for companies who offer visually pleasing goods or services. It is perfect for innovative and captivating ads because of its focus on visual material, stories, and reels. TikTok is excellent for reaching younger audiences and thrives on short-form video content. It is the perfect platform for original and genuine content because of its algorithm, which encourages viral and organic reach.

X (Twitter) is quick, succinct, and excellent for thought leadership, real-time updates, and interacting with your audience directly through hashtags, threads, and tweets.

The Influence of Participation

The foundation of social media marketing is engagement. Starting discussions, establishing connections, and fostering a community around your business are more important than merely publishing material. Engagement entails meaningfully communicating with your audience, like and sharing user-generated material, and replying to comments. Engaging with your followers builds trust and demonstrates your appreciation for their opinions. Respect for one another generates more devoted fans, who are more willing to buy from you. By raising your chances of showing up in users' feeds, gaining momentum, and generating word-of-mouth advertising, engagement increases visibility. Instead of giving a monologue, the goal is to start a conversation.

Developing Your Plan Establishing Specific Objectives: Sales, Traffic, and Awareness

Setting specific, quantifiable goals is the first step in every effective social media marketing effort. You're just sending signals into space if you don't have any aims. Concentrate on three main goals:

Awareness: You want your brand to be known to the public. You may reach a larger audience and demonstrate your worth by introducing your product or service through quality content. Getting people to visit your website, blog, or landing page is the next stage. Here's your chance to highlight your products in further depth and inspire action.

Sales: Conversions are ultimately the result of social media marketing. It involves assisting your audience in moving from awareness to a

decision to buy.
By establishing these specific objectives, you provide the framework for your plan and make it simpler to gauge progress.

Finding Your Target Market

It's critical to understand your audience. Your marketing efforts are like shooting in the dark if you don't know who they are, what they want, and where they spend their time. Determine your target audience's psychographics (interests, habits), demographics (age, gender, geography), and pain issues. To make sure your content appeals to your prospective clients, create buyer personas, which are comprehensive depictions of them. You have a better chance of getting the appropriate message to the right individuals if you are more precise.

Analysis of Competitors:
Take Advice from the Best
Your adversaries are more than simply rivals; they are also important sources of motivation. Determine what they are doing well and what they are not doing well. Examine their client feedback, engagement rates, content style, and social media presence. What is effective for them? What could you do better or differently? You may position your brand for success by taking note of the best practices and finding weaknesses in their approaches. In addition to

identifying possibilities, competitor analysis provides you with the assurance to establish your own niche.

You're positioning yourself for success by being aware of these fundamentals of social media marketing. This is only the start. You will realize social media's full potential as you develop your plan and interact with your audience, turning your presence into a force that produces tangible business outcomes. With the correct strategy, you may achieve remarkable success in the huge, dynamic, and limitless realm of social media marketing.

SECTION 2: PLATFORM-SPECIFIC PROFICIENCY

X (formerly Twitter)

Developing a Loyal Following

The cornerstone of a successful social media marketing approach is cultivating a devoted following on X (previously Twitter). In contrast to other platforms, X benefits greatly from prompt involvement, discussions, and succinct communication. To build a devoted following:

Know Your Niche:

Concentrate on a single issue and often interact with followers about it. Stay focused on a single topic, such as tech developments, business advice, or inspirational material.

Be Consistent: Send out tweets on a regular basis without going overboard. Maintaining visibility without overwhelming your audience may be achieved by posting two to three times each day.

Actively Participate: Tag individuals in pertinent postings, reply to comments, and take part in conversations. Having direct conversations with your followers fosters a feeling of community.

Leverage Lists: To successfully track and interact with your followers, group them into lists (such as influencers, clients, and rivals).

Hashtag Strategy to Go Viral Using hashtags is essential if you want to expand your following. Using popular hashtags or coming up with your own is a terrific strategy to get more exposure on X.

Research Hashtags: **To identify the most appropriate hashtags for your material, use resources such as Hashtagify or X's trending section.**

Be Specific: Use hashtags that are more relevant to your audience's interests rather than ones that are too general and drown your tweet in a sea of content.

Make Your Own Hashtag: **Create a** hashtag that is exclusive to your brand. In addition to encouraging followers to interact with your material, this provides your brand a distinctive character.

Making Money Off of Your X

Presence Making money off of your X presence is a feasible alternative after you have a strong following. The following actions can help you make money from your account:

Affiliate marketing:

Collaborate with companies that appeal to your target

market. To receive a commission, mention their items in your tweets along with affiliate links.

Sponsored Tweets: As you gain popularity, businesses could contact you to advertise their goods and services. One effective strategy to get money from your following is through sponsored content.

Provide Paid Advice or Consultation: If you are an expert in a certain field, use X to provide paid advice or consultations by sending DMs or links to your own website.

Obstacles You Could Face:

Low Engagement: **Concentrate on** improving your content approach if your tweets aren't receiving a lot of interaction. Increase your interaction with other people's tweets, make threads or polls, and make the most of your hashtags.

Algorithm modifications: **Visibility may be impacted by X's frequent algorithm modifications. Keep abreast of current trends and modify your material appropriately to combat this.**

Instagram

Making Scroll-Stopping material
It's crucial to produce material for Instagram that grabs users' attention in a matter of seconds. Here's how to ensure that your posts get noticed:

Instagram is a visual site, so make use of vibrant images. Make use of top-notch photos and videos that capture the essence of your business. Strong black-and-white images or vibrant, colorful photographs stand out.
People enjoy tales, so tell them. Make an effort to provide an emotional hook in your captions as well to keep readers interested.

Try Various Content Types:
To keep your feed interesting and dynamic, try posting carousels, infographics, movies, and GIFs instead of just still photos.
Understanding Reels, Stories, and Posts Every Instagram feature has a certain function. Here's how to utilize them to their fullest:

Reels are the Instagram equivalent of TikTok. Make use of them for brief, visually striking videos. Make an effect by using challenges, popular music, or instructive materials. Stories: Stories are a wonderful method to conduct short surveys or provide behind-the-scenes content because they vanish after 24 hours. Be genuine and don't be scared to display your brand's human side.

Posts: Use posts for information that is more permanent, such product displays or anecdotes. Make sure that each post reflects the style of your business.
Increasing Your Following to 10,000 and Beyond To increase your following from 0 to 10,000,

The secret is consistency: post frequently without going overboard. Try to publish three to five posts a week and at least one Story per day.

Work Together with Influencers: Assemble a team of influencers who share your brand's values. Collaborations can help expose your profile to a wider audience.

Engage and Respond: Always reply to comments and DMs. Show your audience that you value them.

Use Instagram Ads: Invest in targeted ads to grow your account faster. Use Instagram's detailed targeting options to reach people who are most likely to follow and engage with you.

Obstacles You Could Face:

Shadowbanning: If your account is performing poorly, you might have been shadowbanned. To fix this, stop using banned hashtags, engage with followers more, and avoid using bots.

Algorithm Changes: Instagram's algorithm often changes, which can affect visibility. Stay up-to-date and try to mix content types to ensure you're not solely relying on one type of post.

Facebook

Leveraging Groups for Community Building

Facebook groups offer a unique opportunity to foster deeper engagement and build a community around your brand.

Create Your Own Group: Start a Facebook group around your niche. Use it to offer exclusive content, run polls, and provide a platform for discussion.

Be Active in Other Groups: Join groups related to your niche and participate in meaningful discussions. Offer helpful advice, not just promotional content.

Engagement Over Promotion: Focus more on engaging with group members rather than constantly promoting your products. Answer questions, share tips, and ask for feedback.

Paid Ads Demystified Facebook Ads can be intimidating, but once you understand how to use them, they're incredibly effective.

Start with a Small Budget: Test your ads on a small budget first. Facebook allows you to target specific demographics, so use it to your advantage.

Use A/B Testing: Experiment with different visuals, copy, and calls to action to see what works best.

Monitor Results: Facebook's Ads Manager is robust. Use it to track the performance of your ads and adjust your strategy as needed.
Driving Sales Through Facebook Shops Facebook Shops is an amazing way to sell directly from the platform.

Here's how to set it up:

Set Up Your Shop: **Create a Facebook Shop and add your products. Include clear images, detailed descriptions, and pricing.**
Optimize for Mobile: Most Facebook users are on mobile, so make sure your shop looks great on smartphones.

Run Targeted Ads: Once your shop is live, run ads targeting people most likely to buy your products.

Challenges You May Encounter:

Low Engagement in Groups: **If engagement drops, try posting content that encourages interaction, such as polls or direct questions.**

Facebook Ads Not Converting: **If your ads aren't converting, adjust the audience settings, improve your ad copy, and optimize landing pages.**
TikTok

Short-Form Video: **Trends and Challenges TikTok thrives on trends and challenges. Here's how to use them to your advantage:**

Jump on Trends Quickly: **When you spot a trending challenge or sound, act fast! Trends on TikTok move quickly, so timing is everything.**

Add Your Twist: **Don't just mimic the trend; add your unique touch to stand out.**
Use Hashtags: Include popular, relevant hashtags to ensure your videos get discovered by a larger audience.

Becoming a TikTok Influencer

Becoming an influencer on TikTok is about more than just posting videos. Here's how to build your presence:

Find Your Niche: **Whether it's comedy, fitness, cooking, or education, narrow down your niche and be consistent.**

Engage with Your Audience: **Reply to comments and messages. Live streams are also a great way to connect with your followers in real-time.**

Collaborate with Other Creators: **Duets and challenges with other** creators can help you tap into their audience and grow your following.

Earning While Entertaining

Once you start growing, you can begin monetizing your TikTok presence:

Brand Partnerships: **Brands will approach you to promote their products. Negotiate deals that align with your audience.**

Live Gifts: **TikTok allows viewers to send virtual gifts during live streams, which can be exchanged for money.**

Affiliate Marketing: **Promote products and services in your** videos using affiliate links.

Challenges You May Encounter:

Video Not Going Viral: **The TikTok algorithm is unpredictable. Focus on creating high-quality, engaging content consistently to increase your chances.**

Burnout: **TikTok requires frequent uploads. To avoid burnout, batch-create content and schedule posts.**

YouTube

Starting and Growing a Channel in 2025 Starting a YouTube channel in 2025 is easier than ever, but standing out is still a challenge. Here's how to grow:

Find Your Niche: Focus on a topic you're passionate about. Whether it's gaming, DIY, or lifestyle, choosing a niche helps target the right audience you.

Create Consistent Content: Post regularly, ideally once or twice a week. Consistency is key to growing your channel.

Engage with Viewers: Respond to comments and ask for feedback to improve your

content.
Optimizing Videos for Search
and Engagement YouTube is
the second largest search engine
in the world, so optimizing your

content is essential:
Use Keywords in Titles and
Descriptions: Research
keywords related to your content
and include them naturally in
your titles and descriptions.

Engaging Thumbnails: A
compelling thumbnail can
significantly increase your click-
through rate.

Call to Action: Encourage
viewers to like, comment, and
subscribe in every video.
Monetizing Your Content Once

you build a substantial following, here are ways to earn:

Ad Revenue: Once you meet YouTube's eligibility requirements, you can start earning ad revenue.

Affiliate Links: Include affiliate links in your video descriptions to earn commissions on products you recommend. Channel Memberships and

Super Chats: Engage with your audience through live streams and offer perks for paid channel memberships.

Challenges You May Encounter:

Algorithm Changes: **YouTube's algorithm is constantly evolving. Stay up-to-date on best practices and adapt your content accordingly.**

Slow Growth: **Growing a YouTube channel can take time. Focus on producing high-quality content and staying consistent.**

LinkedIn

Establishing Professional Authority LinkedIn is the go-to platform for professionals. Establishing authority involves:

Sharing Valuable Content: **Share insights, articles, and updates that position you as a thought leader in your field.**

Publishing Long-Form Articles: **Write detailed articles that showcase your expertise. These can help establish your credibility.**

Engage with Industry Leaders: **Connect with influencers and experts in your field. Comment** on their posts and share your insights.

Networking That Works

LinkedIn is the best platform for networking:

Personalized Connection Requests: Always send personalized connection requests to people you want to connect with.
Join Relevant Groups: Participate in LinkedIn groups related to your niche and share your knowledge.
Generating Leads on LinkedIn Use LinkedIn's powerful search feature to find potential leads:

Advanced Search: Use LinkedIn's advanced search filters to find people who match

your target audience.
Outreach Campaigns: Craft
personalized messages offering
value, not just promotions.

Challenges You May Encounter:

Low Engagement: **If you're not
getting enough likes or
comments, try posting more
engaging content like polls or
questions.**
Building Connections: **It takes
time to build a strong network
on LinkedIn. Be patient,
consistent, and always offer
value to your connections.**

Pinterest

Visual Marketing for E-Commerce Success Pinterest is all about visual appeal:

Create High-Quality Pins:

Use visually stunning images or infographics for your Pins. Make sure they're high resolution and fit the platform's format.

Optimize Pin Descriptions:

Include keyword-rich descriptions to help your Pins get discovered by users searching for similar content.

Use Rich Pins: These Pins include additional information, such as product details, which can drive more traffic to your

website.
Pinning for Traffic and Sales
Pinterest is a great tool to drive
traffic to your website:

Pin Regularly: Keep your
account active by pinning daily.
Aim for 10-20 Pins per day across
different boards.

Use Pinterest Ads: Pinterest
offers ads that can drive traffic to
your website, increasing sales.
Tools to Automate Your
Pinterest Strategy Use tools to
streamline your Pinterest
marketing:

Tailwind: This scheduling tool
helps you automate Pins and
track analytics.

Canva: Use Canva to create eye-catching Pins easily.

Challenges You May Encounter:

Low Engagement on Pins: **Experiment with different types of Pins (e.g., infographics, tutorials) to see what resonates with your audience.**

Competing for Visibility: **Pinterest is competitive. Use unique keywords and create original, attention-grabbing content. Platform-Specific Mastery**

PART 2 : PLATFORM - SPECIFIC MASR=TERING

X (Formerly Twitter)

Building a Loyal Follower Base
Building a loyal following on X (formerly Twitter) is the foundation of a successful social media marketing strategy. Unlike other platforms, X thrives on concise communication, conversations, and timely engagement. To create a loyal base:

Know Your Niche: Focus on a specific topic and consistently engage with followers on that subject. Whether it's business advice, tech trends, or motivational content, stick to a niche.

Be Consistent: Tweet regularly, but don't overdo it. Posting two to three times a day helps maintain visibility without overwhelming your audience.

Engage Actively: Respond to comments, participate in discussions, and tag people in relevant posts. Engaging directly with your followers creates a sense of community.

Leverage Lists: Organize your followers into lists (e.g., influencers, customers, competitors) to track them effectively and engage meaningfully.

Hashtag Strategy to Go Viral

Hashtags are crucial for reaching beyond your existing follower base. On X, using trending hashtags or creating your own is a great way to increase visibility.

Research Hashtags: Use tools like Hashtagify or X's trending section to find the best hashtags relevant to your content.

Be Specific: Instead of using overly popular hashtags that drown your tweet in a sea of content, opt for more targeted ones that speak directly to your audience's interests.

Create a Brand-Specific Hashtag:
Make your own unique hashtag. This gives your brand a recognizable identity and encourages followers to engage with your content.

Monetizing Your X Presence

Once you have a solid following, monetizing your X presence becomes a viable option. Here are some steps to turn your account into a source of income:

Affiliate Marketing: **Partner with brands relevant to your audience. Share their products in your tweets with affiliate links to earn a commission.**

Sponsored Tweets: **As you grow, companies may approach you to promote their services/products. Sponsored content is a profitable way to earn from your following. Offer Paid Advice or**

Consultation: **If you have expertise in a niche, offer paid consultations or advice directly through X using DMs or links to your personal site.**

Challenges You May Encounter:

Low Engagement: **If your tweets aren't getting much engagement, focus on refining your content strategy. Engage more with others' tweets, create polls or threads, and optimize** your hashtags.

Algorithm Changes: **X's algorithm changes frequently, which can affect visibility. To counteract this, stay updated on the latest trends and adapt your content accordingly.**

Instagram

Creating Scroll-Stopping Content Creating content that captures attention in mere seconds is critical on Instagram.

Here's how to make sure your posts stand out:

Use Vibrant Visuals: **Instagram is a visual platform. Use high-quality images and videos that reflect your brand's personality. Bright, colorful photos or powerful black-and-white shots stand out.**

Tell a Story: **People love stories. Even in your captions, try to weave in an emotional hook that keeps your audience engaged. Experiment with Different**

Content Types: **Don't just post static images—use carousels, infographics, videos, and GIFs to keep your feed fresh and dynamic.**

Mastering Reels, Stories, and Posts Each Instagram feature has its own purpose. Here's how to make the most of them:

Reels: **These are Instagram's answer to TikTok. Use them for short, attention-grabbing videos. Leverage trending sounds, challenges, or educational content to make an impact. Stories: Stories disappear after 24 hours, making them a great way to show behind-the-scenes content or run quick polls. Be authentic and don't be afraid to**

show the human side of your brand.

Posts: For more permanent content, such as product showcases or personal stories, use posts. Ensure that every post aligns with your brand's aesthetic.
Growing Your Account to 10k and Beyond To go from zero to 10k followers:

Consistency is Key: Post regularly but not excessively. Aim for at least 3-5 posts per week and Stories daily.

Collaborate with Influencers: Partner with influencers who resonate with your brand. Collaborations can help expose your profile to a wider audience.

Engage and Respond: Always reply to comments and DMs. Show your audience that you value them.

Use Instagram Ads: Invest in targeted ads to grow your account faster. Use Instagram's detailed targeting options to reach people who are most likely to follow and engage with you.

Challenges You May Encounter:

Shadowbanning: **If your account is performing poorly, you might** have been shadowbanned. To fix this, stop using banned hashtags, engage with followers more, and avoid using bots.

Algorithm Changes: **Instagram's algorithm often changes, which can affect visibility. Stay up-to-date and try to mix content types to ensure you're not solely relying on one type of post.**

Facebook

Leveraging Groups for Community Building Facebook groups offer a unique opportunity to foster deeper engagement and build a community around your brand.

Create Your Own Group: Start a Facebook group around your niche. Use it to offer exclusive content, run polls, and provide a platform for discussion.

Be Active in Other Groups: Join groups related to your niche and participate in meaningful discussions. Offer helpful advice, not just promotional content.

Engagement Over

Promotion: Focus more on engaging with group members rather than constantly promoting your products. Answer questions, share tips, and ask for feedback.

Paid Ads Demystified Facebook Ads can be intimidating, but once you understand how to use them, they're incredibly effective.

Start with a Small Budget: Test your ads on a small budget first. Facebook allows you to target specific demographics, so use it to your advantage.

Use A/B Testing: Experiment with different visuals, copy, and calls to action to see what works best.

Monitor Results: **Facebook's Ads Manager is robust. Use it to track the performance of your ads and adjust your strategy as needed.**
Driving Sales Through Facebook Shops Facebook Shops is an amazing way to sell directly from the platform.

Here's how to set it up:

Set Up Your Shop: **Create a Facebook Shop and add your products. Include clear images, detailed descriptions, and pricing.**

Optimize for Mobile: **Most Facebook users are on mobile, so make sure your shop looks great on smartphones.**

Run Targeted Ads: Once your shop is live, run ads targeting people most likely to buy your products.

Challenges You May Encounter:

Low Engagement in Groups: **If** engagement drops, try posting content that encourages interaction, such as polls or direct questions.

Facebook Ads Not Converting: **If** your ads aren't converting, adjust the audience settings, improve your ad copy, and optimize landing pages.

TikTok

Short-Form Video: Trends and Challenges TikTok thrives on trends and challenges. Here's how to use them to your advantage:

Jump on Trends Quickly: When you spot a trending challenge or sound, act fast! Trends on TikTok move quickly, so timing is everything.

Add Your Twist: Don't just mimic the trend; add your unique touch to stand out. Use Hashtags: Include popular, relevant hashtags to ensure your videos get discovered by a larger audience.

Becoming a TikTok Influencer Becoming an influencer on TikTok is about more than just posting videos. Here's how to build your presence:

Find Your Niche: **Whether it's comedy, fitness, cooking, or education, narrow down your niche and be consistent.**

Engage with Your Audience: **Reply to comments and messages. Live streams are also a great way to connect with your followers in real-time.**

Collaborate with Other Creators: **Duets and challenges with other creators can help you tap into** their audience and grow your following.

Earning While Entertaining
Once you start growing, you can begin monetizing your TikTok presence:

Brand Partnerships: **Brands will approach you to promote their products. Negotiate deals that align with your audience.**

Live Gifts: **TikTok allows viewers to send virtual gifts during live streams, which can be exchanged for money.**

Affiliate Marketing: **Promote products and services in your videos using affiliate links.**

Challenges You May Encounter:

Video Not Going Viral: **The TikTok algorithm is unpredictable. Focus on creating high-quality, engaging content consistently to increase your chances.**

Burnout: **TikTok requires frequent uploads. To avoid burnout, batch-create content and schedule posts.**

YouTube

Starting and Growing a Channel in 2025 Starting a YouTube channel in 2025 is easier than ever, but standing out is still a challenge. Here's how to grow:

Find Your Niche: **Focus on a topic you're passionate about. Whether it's gaming, DIY, or lifestyle, choosing a niche helps you target the right audience.**

Create Consistent Content: **Post regularly, ideally once or twice a week. Consistency is key to growing your channel.**

Engage with Viewers: **Respond to comments and ask for feedback to improve your content.**

Optimizing Videos for Search and Engagement YouTube is the second largest search engine in the world, so optimizing your content is essential:

Use Keywords in Titles and Descriptions: Research keywords related to your content and include them naturally in your titles and descriptions. *Engaging Thumbnails:* **A** compelling thumbnail can significantly increase your click-through rate.

Call to Action: **Encourage viewers** to like, comment, and subscribe in every video.
Monetizing Your Content Once you build a substantial following, here are ways to earn:

Ad Revenue: **Once you meet YouTube's eligibility requirements, you can start earning ad revenue.**

Affiliate Links: **Include affiliate links in your video descriptions to earn commissions on products you recommend.**

Channel Memberships and Super Chats: **Engage with your audience through live streams and offer perks for paid channel memberships.**

Challenges You May Encounter:

Algorithm Changes: **YouTube's**

algorithm is constantly evolving. Stay up-to-date on best practices and adapt your content accordingly.

Slow Growth: **Growing a YouTube channel can take time. Focus on producing high-quality content and staying consistent.**

LinkedIn

Establishing Professional Authority LinkedIn is the go-to platform for professionals. Establishing authority involves:

Sharing Valuable Content: **Share insights, articles, and updates that position you as a thought leader in your field.**

Publishing Long-Form Articles: **Write detailed articles that showcase your expertise. These can help establish your credibility.**

Engage with Industry Leaders: **Connect with influencers and experts in your field. Comment on their posts and share your** insights.

Networking That Works **LinkedIn is the best platform for networking:**

Personalized Connection Requests: Always send personalized connection requests to people you want to connect with.

Join Relevant Groups: Participate in LinkedIn groups related to your niche and share your knowledge.

Generating Leads on LinkedIn Use LinkedIn's powerful search feature to find potential leads:

Advanced Search: Use LinkedIn's advanced search filters to find people who match your target audience.

Outreach Campaigns: Craft

personalized messages offering value, not just promotions.

Challenges You May Encounter:

Low Engagement: **If you're not getting enough likes or comments, try posting more engaging content like polls or questions.**

Building Connections: **It takes time to build a strong network on LinkedIn. Be patient, consistent, and always offer value to your connections.**

Pinterest

Visual Marketing for E-Commerce Success Pinterest is all about visual appeal:

Create High-Quality Pins: **Use visually stunning images or infographics for your Pins. Make sure they're high resolution and fit the platform's format.**

Optimize Pin Descriptions: **Include keyword-rich descriptions to help your Pins get discovered by users searching for similar content.**

Use Rich Pins: **These Pins include additional information, such as product details, which can drive more traffic to your website. Pinning for Traffic and Sales**

Pinterest is a great tool to drive traffic to your website:

Pin Regularly: Keep your account active by pinning daily. Aim for 10-20 Pins per day across different boards.

Use Pinterest Ads: Pinterest offers ads that can drive traffic to your website, increasing sales. Tools to Automate Your

Pinterest Strategy Use tools to streamline your Pinterest marketing:

Tailwind: This scheduling tool helps you automate Pins and track analytics.

Canva: Use Canva to create eye-catching Pins easily.

Challenges You May Encounter:

Low Engagement on Pins: **Experiment with different types of Pins (e.g., infographics, tutorials) to see what resonates with your audience.**

Competing for Visibility: **Pinterest is competitive. Use unique keywords and create original, attention-grabbing content.**

SECTION 3: THE ANATOMY OF VIRAL CONTENT

Content Is King

Content is the lifeblood of your plan in the dynamic realm of social media. In addition to capturing attention, great content encourages interaction, establishes credibility, and converts infrequent visitors into devoted fans. Let's examine what constitutes shareable material, the role that emotional triggers play, and successful ways to exploit user-generated content.

What Qualifies as Shareable Content?

When content solves a problem, has great value, or strikes an emotional chord, it becomes viral. Here's how to create content that people want to share:

Activate Universal Feelings:
Tell a narrative to make others happy, surprised, or even nostalgic. Stories that evoke strong feelings are more likely to be shared.
Example: On social media sites like Facebook and Instagram, a moving transformation narrative accompanied by images may do wonders.

Provide Value:
Quick tips or "how-to" instructions are examples of

educational content that frequently get more shares. Trick: To draw in viewers and promote sharing, provide snackable advice in your lengthier films on YouTube.

Promote Communication:
Engagement is increased by content with a clear call to action (e.g., "Tag a friend who needs this!").
Platform-Specific Hack: To increase visibility on TikTok, invite fans to duet or remix your clip.
Timing and Emotional Triggers Emotions and timing are crucial for social media success:

Find the Best Times to Post:

To find out when your audience is most engaged, use analytics tools.

Hack: Instagram works best in the nights, whereas LinkedIn is best for professional material in the mornings.

Emotional Reaction Triggers:

Surprise: To keep readers interested, incorporate surprising turns or revelations into your writing.

Empathy: To establish a personal connection, share your struggles and victories from real life.

Take Advantage of Trends:

For increased visibility, produce

material centered on challenges or popular hashtags.

Hack: If you want to swiftly profit from hot themes, TikTok's "Discover" feature is your best buddy.

Making Use of User-Generated Content

User-generated content (UGC) builds confidence and is genuine:

Promote user-generated content: Organize competitions where fans post images or videos of themselves utilizing your goods or services.

Hack: To promote engagement on Instagram, provide rewards like shout-outs or discounts.

Fans of Features:

Sharing material produced by fans builds community and gives followers a sense of worth. For instance, make boards on Pinterest devoted to user-generated content for brand merchandise.

Hashtag Initiatives:

Make original hashtags to monitor and highlight user-submitted content.

Hack: **To help content trend, use branded hashtags for campaigns on X and Twitter.**

Creating Content on a Budget

High-quality content creation doesn't have to be expensive:

Utilize Low-Cost and Free Tools:
Great beginning tools include Grammarly for perfect captions, CapCut for video editing, and Canva for visuals.
Hack: To improve your videos on YouTube without worrying about copyright, utilize free music sources.

Creation of Content in Batches:
Set aside a day to produce and plan many pieces of content for the next week.

Hack: **To effectively plan articles across several sites, use tools like Buffer or Hootsuite.**

Keep Yourself Consistent: To guarantee visual coherence, make content templates for Instagram posts, reels, and stories.

Hack: Use programs like Tailwind to automate your Pinterest pinning routine. Automation and Scheduling Maintaining engagement requires consistency, and automation may streamline your process:

The Greatest Time-Saving Tools:

To pre-schedule your postings,

use programs like Later, Planoly, or Creator Studio.

Hack: Make use of LinkedIn's scheduling tools to maintain audience interest outside of business hours.

How Frequently to Post on Every Site:

Instagram: three to five times a week, with stories every day.
X (Twitter): Frequently throughout the day for maximum exposure.

TikTok: To keep up with trends, post one to three times a day.
Trick: Pay more attention to quality than quantity. Posting

once with effect is preferable to posting mediocrely several times.

Handling Several Accounts:
To easily manage information across platforms, use social media dashboards.
Hack: **Repurpose information to strengthen your approach. You may use a TikTok video again as a YouTube short and an Instagram reel.**

Motivation and Reaching Objectives
Clarity and commitment are necessary to reach your social media objectives:

Establish Specific,

Achievable Goals:

Establish clear goals, such as acquiring 10,000 followers or a 30% increase in interaction within three months.
Hack: **Divide these objectives into more manageable benchmarks and acknowledge each accomplishment.**

Monitor Your Progress:

Utilize analytics to track results and improve your approach. For instance, Instagram Insights may show you what kinds of material your audience is interested in.
Adjust and Develop:

Although algorithms evolve, you

may stay ahead of them by using your imagination.

Hack: **Keep up of platform developments and take use of new features, such as Instagram's improved AI tools or X's extended post possibilities.**

SECTION 4: ADVERTISING AND ANALYTICS

Unlocking Your Social Media Potential

In 2025, advertising and analytics are not just tools—they're the keys to achieving unparalleled success on social media. Whether you're a beginner aiming to make your mark or a seasoned marketer looking to refine your approach, mastering paid advertising and analytics will propel your social media campaigns to new heights. Let's dive into this transformative journey with actionable insights and proven strategies.

Paid Advertising 101

Choosing the Right Platform for Ads

Every social media platform caters to a unique audience. The secret to advertising success lies in aligning your goals with the platform that suits your target demographic:

- *X (Formerly Twitter):* **Ideal for real-time engagement and brand visibility. Use promoted tweets to drive awareness during trending moments or events.**

- *Instagram:* **Perfect for visual brands. Leverage Instagram Stories and Reels Ads to** showcase products in a dynamic, engaging format.

- *Facebook:* **With detailed targeting options, Facebook is the go-to for connecting with niche audiences. Use carousel ads for multi-product displays.**

- *TikTok:* **Best for brands targeting younger audiences. Create entertaining and authentic ads that blend seamlessly with organic content.**

- **YouTube: The powerhouse of video marketing. Invest in skippable in-stream ads to captivate viewers within seconds.**

- *LinkedIn:* **The ultimate platform for B2B marketing.**

Use sponsored posts to reach decision-makers and professionals.

Goal: **Define your audience's behavior and match it with the platform where they spend the most time.**

Creating High-Converting Campaigns

High-converting campaigns share common traits:

- *Compelling Visuals:* **Use vibrant, eye-catching graphics and videos. For example, TikTok thrives on creativity, so embrace trends and challenges.**

- *Clear Call-to-Action (CTA):* **Guide your audience with actionable prompts like**

"Shop Now" or "Learn More."

- *Personalization:* **Tailor your message to resonate with specific segments. Facebook and LinkedIn allow advanced targeting for precise outreach.**

- *Mobile Optimization:* **Ensure all ads are optimized for mobile devices, as over 70% of users access social media on phones.**

Hack: **Use A/B testing to refine ad creatives and CTAs for maximum impact.**

Measuring ROI and Scaling Your Ads

Your advertising efforts must deliver measurable results. Here's how to ensure your return on investment (ROI) is optimized:

- *Track Key Metrics:* **Monitor metrics such as click-through rates (CTR), cost-per-click (CPC), and conversion rates. Platforms like Facebook Ads Manager and Google Analytics simplify tracking.**

- *Identify Winning Ads:* **Double down on ads that perform well. Scale by increasing your budget for high-performing campaigns.**

- *Refine Underperformers:* **Use analytics to pinpoint weak links—whether it's the creative, audience targeting, or CTA—and adjust accordingly.**

Goal: Adopt a continuous improvement mindset to maximize ROI and scale effectively.

Understanding Analytics
Key Metrics to Track Success

Analytics is the backbone of any successful social media strategy. Here's what you need to track:

- *Engagement Rate:* **Measure likes, comments, shares, and saves. High engagement indicates resonant content.**

- *Reach and Impressions:* **Understand how many people saw your content and how often.**

- *Conversion Rate:* **Track how many users completed the desired action (purchase, sign-up, etc.).**

Hack: **Use native tools like Instagram Insights and LinkedIn Analytics for quick overviews. For deeper insights, invest in platforms like Hootsuite or Sprout Social.**

Using Insights to Optimize Strategy

Analytics provides a roadmap for continuous improvement:

- *Identify Patterns:* **Look for trends in high-performing posts and replicate their elements.**

- *Understand Audience Behavior:* **Discover peak**

activity times and schedule posts accordingly.

- *Tweak Your Approach:* **If a campaign isn't performing, adjust variables like audience demographics or ad placement.**

Goal: **Develop a data-driven approach that evolves with your audience's preferences.**

Case Studies: Learning from Data

Real-life examples inspire actionable strategies:

- *TikTok Ads:* **A small clothing brand used viral challenges to increase sales by 400% in a month. They analyzed trending hashtags and created relatable, user-friendly content.**

- *Instagram Stories Ads:* **A fitness trainer targeted users interested in home workouts, driving 5,000 course sign-ups in a week. Insights from Instagram Analytics helped refine the CTA.**

- *LinkedIn Sponsored Posts:* **A software company secured 20 B2B clients by sharing thought leadership articles targeting decision-makers.**

Hack: **Study competitors' campaigns and adapt their winning strategies to your niche.**

Achieving Your Goals on Each Platform

X (Twitter): **Consistency is king. Post daily, engage with** followers, and amplify reach using trending hashtags.

Instagram: **Showcase authenticity. Use Stories to share behind-the-scenes moments and Reels to tap into trending audio.**

Facebook: **Build community through Groups and use retargeting ads to convert warm leads.**

YouTube: **Optimize videos for search with compelling thumbnails and keywords. Collaborate with other creators for cross-promotion.**

LinkedIn: **Share industry insights and participate in discussions to position yourself as a thought leader.**

TikTok: **Prioritize trends and keep content fun, fast, and engaging. Respond to comments to increase interaction.**

SECTION 5: IMPROVE YOUR SOCIAL MEDIA MARKETING IN 2025 WITH THESE GROWTH HACKS AND TRENDS

2025's Top 10 Growth Hacks

Social media platforms change quickly, so using creative tactics to remain ahead of the curve is essential. You will stand out thanks to these best growth tactics, which guarantee steady progress and achievement.

Current Effective Strategies

Authenticity and user involvement are still crucial for social media success in 2025.

Hack: **To get attention fast, use micro-content, which are brief but powerful pieces like Instagram Reels or TikTok films.**

Objective: **Establish sincere relationships by answering each mention, DM, and remark.**

Execution: **Determine when to post and create content that speaks to the interests of your audience by using platform statistics.**

Pro Tip: **To make your material relevant, concentrate on delivering a compelling tale. Provide testimonies, behind-the-scenes looks, or inspirational** tales.

Using AI in Marketing

Artificial intelligence is today a part of marketing, not the future.

Hack: **Make use of AI technologies for analytics, scheduling, and content creation. Platforms such as Jasper AI (for automation) and ChatGPT (for copywriting) are revolutionary.**

Objective: **Deliver individualized content at scale while increasing accuracy and efficiency.**

Execution: **To keep your campaigns ahead of the curve, use AI-driven insights to forecast** trends and audience behavior.

Pro Tip: **To strike a balance between efficiency and connection, automate answers to frequently asked questions while retaining a human touch for more complicated inquiries.**

Forming Alliances with Influencers

Although influencer marketing is still quite popular, the strategy has changed to put authenticity first.

Hack: **Work together with micro-influencers in your field who have a large following.**

Objective: **Encourage audience trust and focused engagement.**

Execution: **Create enduring alliances rather than sporadic initiatives. Collaborate to produce content that complements the influencer's style and your business.**

Pro Tip: **To identify partners and monitor campaign effectiveness, use influencer platforms such as AspireIQ.**

New Developments in Social Media

In 2025, social media is all about flexibility. You may succeed and ride the tide of change with the support of these trends.

Trending Topics for 2025

Platforms such as YouTube Shorts, Instagram Reels, and TikTok continue to rule the short-form video content market.

Interactive content: **AR filters, polls, and quizzes all creatively engage users.**

Social commerce: **It's easier than ever to shop from within social media networks.**

Objective: **Adopt these trends early to stay relevant.**

Execution: **Set aside some time in your content plan to test out novel features, such as TikTok LIVE shopping events or**

Instagram collabs.

Pro Tip: **Keep abreast of platform announcements to get an advantage over your competitors by being the first to utilize new features.**

Getting Ready for the Upcoming Major Change

Although the social media world is uncertain, you can prepare your plan for the future.

Hack: **To reduce the danger of algorithm modifications or platform-specific downturns, diversify your presence across several platforms.**

Objective: **Establish a robust web presence that prospers despite** changes in the industry. Execution: Start establishing a presence by identifying new features or platforms early on, such as Web3 social networks or metaverse integration.

Pro Tip: **Set aside time each week for study and experimentation; take advantage of webinars, test out new platforms, and speak with professionals in the field.**

Keeping Up with the Times

You have to lead the group in addition to keeping up if you want to succeed.

Hack: **Keep an eye on global trends and analyze your competition to continuously learn and adapt.**

Objective: **Predict changes in customer behavior and make proactive adjustments to your tactics.**

Execution: **To keep up with the latest discussions and themes in your niche, use resources like BuzzSumo or Google Trends.**

Pro Tip: **Participate in online forums or communities where innovators and thought leaders talk about the direction of social media marketing.**

Platform-Specific Objectives and Techniques

Every platform has different chances for development and success. Here's how to make the

most of your influence:

To increase discoverability, incorporate hashtags and popular sounds into Reels.
Use the "Collab" function to work together on postings with other authors.

Engage with viral trends and post frequently (three to five times per day).
TikTok's "Spark Ads" may be used to promote successful organic content.

For improved SEO, use chapter markers when creating long-

form material.
Pay attention to YouTube Shorts
to swiftly expand your following.

X on Twitter:
Use pertinent hashtags to
participate in popular
discussions.
Engage audiences in real-time
communication by using
"Twitter Spaces."

LinkedIn:
Distribute thought-provoking
articles with practical advice.
Participate in LinkedIn groups
to build credibility in your field.

The Way to Achievement
You can maintain your lead in
the cutthroat field of social

media marketing by implementing these growth hacks and trends. In addition to improving your approach, persistent experimenting, utilizing AI, and embracing new trends will position you as a leader in the industry.

SECTION 6:DIFFICULTIES AND SOLUTIONS

Avoiding Typical Social Media Marketing Mistakes

Social media marketing is a dynamic, ever-evolving field that demands creativity, resilience, and adaptability. As you navigate this exciting yet competitive landscape, challenges like algorithm changes, burnout, account security, and managing negative feedback are inevitable. These challenges may, however, be turned into chances for success and development with the correct attitude, resources, and tactics. Together with practical tips to help you accomplish your objectives on various social media platforms, let's take a closer look at these issues and their fixes.

Handling Modifications to Algorithms

When and how your material is seen by your audience is decided by algorithms. Although they might be annoying, changes are meant to enhance the user experience. It is essential to comprehend these developments and adjust accordingly.

The fix and workarounds:

Stay Updated: **Regularly follow platform blogs (e.g., Meta, YouTube Creator Blog) and** influencer marketing sites to understand the latest updates.

Take Part in Meaningful

Activities: **Sincere interaction is rewarded by algorithms. Focus on creating interactive posts that prompt comments, shares, and saves.**

Diversify Your Content: **Use a mix of content formats like reels, carousels, stories, and live videos to maximize reach.**

Platform-Specific Goal Hacks:

Instagram: **Post at peak times and leverage trending audio for reels.**

YouTube:

Optimize video titles and descriptions with trending keywords.

TikTok: Consistently jump on trends while tailoring them to your niche.

Avoiding Burnout and Staying Consistent

The pressure to create engaging content can be overwhelming. Without balance, burnout can affect creativity and productivity.

The fix and workarounds:

Set Realistic Goals: Focus on quality over quantity. Plan for 3-5 impactful posts per week instead of daily uploads.

Batch Create Content: **Dedicate a few hours weekly to creating multiple posts, ensuring you have a steady stream of content without daily stress.**

Automate Scheduling: **Tools like Buffer, Hootsuite, or Later can handle posting while you focus on strategy.**
Take Breaks: **Regular digital detoxes refresh your mind and spark creativity.**

Platform-Specific Goal Hacks:

LinkedIn: **Share thought leadership posts bi-weekly to maintain professional**

engagement.
Pinterest: Schedule pins months in advance for evergreen traffic.

Protecting Your Accounts from Hacks

Cybersecurity threats are on the rise, and losing control of your account can severely damage your reputation.

Solution and Hacks:

Enable Two-Factor Authentication (2FA): Ensure that all accounts have 2FA enabled for an added layer of security.

Use Strong Passwords: Avoid predictable passwords; instead, use password managers for unique, complex combinations. Regular Backups: Maintain a backup of your content and follower data to mitigate potential losses.

Stay Vigilant: **Be cautious of phishing attempts or suspicious links sent via DMs or emails.**

Platform-Specific Goal Hacks:

Facebook: **Regularly check your account's activity log for unauthorized access.**

X (Twitter): **Use tools like TweetDeck for account management without sharing passwords.**

Handling Negative Feedback and Crisis

Social media invites a mix of praise and criticism. Handling negative feedback effectively can transform challenges into opportunities to strengthen your brand.

Solution and Hacks:

Respond with Grace:
Acknowledge the feedback without being defensive. Show empathy and a willingness to address concerns.

Take Criticism Offline: **For serious complaints, direct conversations to private messages for resolution.**

Leverage Criticism for Growth:
Use feedback to identify areas for improvement in your product or service.

Showcase Positive Responses:
Highlight how you've resolved issues to demonstrate transparency and reliability.

Platform-Specific Goal Hacks:

YouTube: **Reply to negative comments with constructive solutions and pin positive testimonials to foster community trust.**

TikTok: **Create a fun, engaging response to a critical comment, showcasing authenticity.**

Inspiring Path to Success Across Platforms

Achieving your social media goals isn't just about overcoming challenges—it's about using them to fuel your growth. Here's how:

Instagram: **Build a strong personal brand by blending relatable stories with aspirational content. Engage authentically with your audience through polls, Q&A, and live sessions.**

YouTube: **Prioritize consistent uploads with actionable, value-driven content. Optimize videos with keywords, thumbnails, and calls to action for maximum impact.**

Facebook: **Utilize groups to**

foster a loyal community. Post regularly with a mix of user-generated content and educational posts.

LinkedIn: **Establish authority by sharing case studies, articles, and professional insights. Collaborate with industry leaders for mutual growth.**

TikTok: **Use humor and relatability to capture attention. Consistently align your content with trending challenges and music while maintaining brand identity.**

Monetizing Your Efforts: Unlocking the Power of Social Media

Social media platforms are more than simply instruments for connecting; they lead to financial freedom and economic success. Monetizing your social media presence needs smart thinking, innovation, and perseverance. Below, we'll go over how to generate several money streams, particular monetization approaches, and platform-specific tricks for optimizing your potential.

Creating Multiple Income Streams.

Diversification is the gold

standard of modern entrepreneurship. Relying on a single source of income exposes you to risk, but diversifying your income creates a safety net and exponential development prospects.

Affiliate Marketing

Affiliate marketing is a win-win situation in which you earn a commission by advertising products or services.

How to Start:

Select items that are relevant to your niche and audience.
Join affiliate programs such as Amazon Associates, ClickBank, and ShareASale.
Create honest, interesting

material about these items (such as reviews and tutorials).

Platform Hacks:

Instagram: Use Stories and Reels to highlight items with swipe-up affiliate links.

YouTube: Include affiliate links in video descriptions, along with how-to tips.

TikTok: Make short, catchy videos that demonstrate how a product solves a problem.

Selling Digital Products and Courses.

Digital items like as eBooks,

templates, and online courses are both scalable and profitable.

How to Start:

Identify your target audience's demands.
Create high-quality content with apps like Canva or Teachable.
Promote your items with email campaigns and social media advertisements.

Platform Hacks:

X (Twitter): **Use threads to share free tips that lead to your premium course.**

Pinterest: **Pin pictures of your items that connect to a landing** page.

LinkedIn: **Share case studies or success stories related to your course.**

Sponsorship and Partnerships

Partnering with businesses allows you to earn while promoting things that you believe in.

How to Start:

Create a media kit using your audience demographics and engagement stats.
Pitch to firms that fit your specialization or join platforms such as Aspire or Upfluence.

Be genuine—brands respect influencers who truly connect with their goods.

Platform Hacks:

Instagram: **Use the hashtag #ad to highlight sponsored content in Stories and Feed posts.**

YouTube: **Incorporate advertisers easily into your content without offending viewers.**

TikTok: **Use trends to generate relatable sponsored content.**

Creating a Personal Brand
A strong personal brand establishes you as an expert in your field, generating both

opportunities and loyalty.

Become the go-to expert in your niche.

How to Start:

Define your specialty and specialization clearly.
Share high-quality, consistent material that solves issues.
Use comments and direct messages to truly engage with your audience.

Platform Hacks:

LinkedIn: **Create thought-provoking articles to build credibility.**

Facebook: **Hold live Q&A sessions to interact with your audience.
Create instructive playlists on YouTube to showcase your knowledge.
Leveraging Media and Speaking Opportunities
Public appearances and media coverage increase your visibility and reputation.**

How to Start:

**Consider appearing as a guest speaker on podcasts, seminars, or events.
Use services such as HARO (Help a Reporter Out) to seek media chances.
Share milestones and accomplishments on social**

media.

Platform Hacks:

X (Twitter): **Create threads to share your trip and insights, and tag important media sites. Instagram: Share stories or carousels of behind-the-scenes preparation for speaking engagements.**

LinkedIn: **Publicize your media appearances to build professional relationships. Long-term strategies for passive income. Creating evergreen content and utilizing automation are critical to sustaining money over time.**

How to Start:

Create a library of timeless materials (such as eBooks and online courses).
Use platforms such as Mailchimp to automate email marketing funnels.
Invest in SEO for steady organic visitors.

Platform Hacks:

Pinterest: **Use Tailwind to plan evergreen content to ensure consistent traffic.**
YouTube: Concentrate on tutorial videos that will be relevant for years.

Instagram: **Use Highlights to make valuable material more accessible.**

Inspiration to Take Action
Imagine creating a life in which your passion provides cash while also benefiting others. Social media is more than simply likes and follows; it's about adding value, solving issues, and having an influence.

Steps to Achieve Your Goals
Start Small but Dream Big: Begin with one income stream and expand over time.
Stay Consistent: Success comes from showing up daily with authentic content.
Invest in Yourself: Learn continuously about trends, tools, and techniques.

Engage and Evolve: Your audience and platforms evolve; adapt to stay relevant.
By following these strategies and leveraging platform-specific hacks, your journey toward financial freedom and social media success in 2025 will not only be achievable but incredibly rewarding.

MONETIZING YOUR EFFORTS:

Unlocking the Power of Social Media

Social media platforms are more than simply instruments for connecting; they lead to financial freedom and economic success. Monetizing your social media presence needs smart thinking, innovation, and perseverance. Below, we'll go over how to generate several money streams, particular monetization approaches, and platform-specific tricks for optimizing your potential.

Creating Multiple Income Streams.
Diversification is the gold standard of modern entrepreneurship. Relying on a single source of income exposes you to risk, but diversifying your income creates a safety net and exponential development prospects.

Affiliate Marketing
Affiliate marketing is a win-win situation in which you earn a commission by advertising products or services.

How to Start:

Select items that are relevant to your niche and audience.
Join affiliate programs such as

Amazon Associates, ClickBank, and ShareASale.
Create honest, interesting material about these items (such as reviews and tutorials).

Platform Hacks:

Instagram: **Use Stories and Reels to highlight items with swipe-up affiliate links.**

YouTube: **Include affiliate links in video descriptions, along with how-to tips.**

TikTok: **Make short, catchy videos that demonstrate how a product solves a problem.**
Selling Digital Products and Courses.

Digital items like as eBooks, templates, and online courses are both scalable and profitable.

How to Start:

Identify your target audience's demands.
Create high-quality content with apps like Canva or Teachable.
Promote your items with email campaigns and social media advertisements.

Platform Hacks:

X (Twitter): Use threads to share free tips that lead to your premium course.
Pinterest: Pin pictures of your items that connect to a landing page.

LinkedIn: **Share case studies or success stories related to your course.**

Sponsorship and Partnerships

Partnering with businesses allows you to earn while promoting things that you believe in.

How to Start:

**Create a media kit using your audience demographics and engagement stats.
Pitch to firms that fit your specialization or join platforms such as Aspire or Upfluence.
Be genuine—brands respect influencers who truly connect with their goods.**

Platform Hacks:

Instagram: Use the hashtag #ad to highlight sponsored content in Stories and Feed posts.

YouTube: Incorporate advertisers easily into your content without offending viewers.

TikTok: Use trends to generate relatable sponsored content.

Creating a Personal Brand
A strong personal brand establishes you as an expert in your field, generating both opportunities and loyalty.

Become the go-to expert in your niche.

How to Start:

Define your specialty and specialization clearly.
Share high-quality, consistent material that solves issues.
Use comments and direct messages to truly engage with your audience.
Platform Hacks:

LinkedIn: Create thought-provoking articles to build credibility.

Facebook: **Hold live Q&A** sessions to interact with your audience.
Create instructive playlists on YouTube to showcase your knowledge.

Leveraging Media and Speaking Opportunities

Public appearances and media coverage increase your visibility and reputation.

How to Start:

Consider appearing as a guest speaker on podcasts, seminars, or events.
Use services such as **HARO (Help a Reporter Out)** to seek media chances.
Share milestones and accomplishments on social media.

Platform Hacks:

X (Twitter): **Create threads to share your trip and insights, and** tag important media sites. Instagram: Share stories or carousels of behind-the-scenes preparation for speaking engagements.

LinkedIn: **Publicize your media appearances to build professional relationships.**

Long-term strategies for passive income.
Creating evergreen content and utilizing automation are critical to sustaining money over time.

How to Start:

Create a library of timeless materials (such as eBooks and online courses).

Use platforms such as
Mailchimp to automate email
marketing funnels.
Invest in **SEO** for steady organic
visitors.

Platform Hacks:

Pinterest: **Use Tailwind to plan
evergreen content to ensure
consistent traffic.**

YouTube: **Concentrate on tutorial
videos that will be relevant for
years.**

Instagram: **Use Highlights to
make valuable material more
accessible.**

Inspiration to Take Action

Imagine creating a life in which your passion provides cash while also benefiting others. Social media is more than simply likes and follows; it's about adding value, solving issues, and having an influence.

Steps to Achieving Your Goals

Start Small, but Dream Big: Begin with a single source of income and gradually increase.

Stay Consistent: Success is achieved by providing real information on a regular basis.

Invest in yourself. Continue to learn about new trends, tools, and strategies.

Engage and evolve: Your audience and platforms change;

adapt to remain relevant. Following these methods and exploiting platform-specific hacks will not only make your trip to financial independence and social media success in 2025 possible, but also extremely satisfying.

CONCLUSION

As we conclude our transforming trip through the Social Media Marketing Guide 2025, let us review the main factors that will propel you from novice to expert.

Recap: Your Plan for Success Your success in social media marketing is dependent on knowing the fundamentals, adjusting to platform-specific methods, and exploiting cutting-edge technologies. We've taken down each platform—X, Instagram, Facebook, TikTok, YouTube, LinkedIn, and Pinterest—and provided concrete advice for growing your following, creating compelling content, and monetizing efficiently. Your plan is now complete: a clear path for transforming ideas into influence and followers into devoted champions.

The Journey Ahead: Remaining Relevant in 2025

Social media is always developing, and being relevant needs you to:

Continue Learning: Stay current on platform upgrades and new trends.

Be adaptable: Embrace change and explore new tactics without fear.

Engage Authentically: Develop genuine relationships with your audience to foster trust.

This book has given you the

skills you need to effectively navigate the waves of change.

Your First Steps to Social Media Marketing Mastery.

Start small yet smart:

Choose the platform where your target audience is most engaged.

Focus on producing high-quality, consistent material.

Engage every day by responding to comments, following new accounts, and networking with peers.

Use the ideas and strategies in this guide to optimize and grow. Success is not a sprint, but a marathon. Take action now.

Bonus Resources: Free Templates and Checklists. Streamline your productivity with actionable templates for content calendars, marketing campaigns, and analytics reporting. These tools are intended to save time and maintain uniformity.

Recommended Tools and Platforms

Enhance your productivity using scheduling (like Hootsuite), design (like Canva), and analytics (like Sprout Social). Even if you're just starting out, these platforms will help you attain professional outcomes.

Inspirational Success Stories Discover how everyday people

transformed become social media sensations. From a small-town baker selling internationally via Instagram to a YouTube producer earning six figures through niche content, their experiences demonstrate that success is only one step away: continuous action.

Make your mark. The world is eager to witness your genius!

www.ingramcontent.com/pod-product-compliance
Lightning Source LLC
LaVergne TN
LVHW051340050326
832903LV00031B/3659

Your Shortcut to Social Media Success in 2025!

Are you ready to turn your passion into profit and build a thriving online presence? This book is your ultimate roadmap to mastering social media, whether you're a total beginner or looking to take your strategy to the next level.

Inside, you'll discover:

Platform-specific strategies for Instagram, TikTok, YouTube, Facebook, LinkedIn, X (formerly Twitter), and Pinterest.
Growth hacks to boost followers, engagement, and visibility.
Proven monetization methods to turn likes into income streams.
Step-by-step guides to create content, beat algorithms, and scale your influence.
AI-powered tools and 2025's top marketing trends to stay ahead.

No fluff, no jargon—just actionable strategies to grow your audience, build your brand, and make money doing what you love. If you're serious about succeeding in today's digital world, this book will give you the tools to make it happen.